First hundred words in Chinese

Heather Amery

Illustrated by Stephen Cartwright

Translation and pronunciation guide by
Quarto Translations

Designed by Mike Olley and Jan McCafferty

 There is a little yellow duck to find in every picture.

客厅 *kè tīng*　The living room

爸爸　*bà ba*　Daddy

妈妈　*mā ma*　Mummy

男孩　*nán hái*　boy

女孩
nǚ hái girl

婴儿
yīng ér baby

狗
gǒu dog

猫
māo cat

3

衣服 *yī fu* Clothes

鞋
xié shoes

内裤
nèi kù pants

套头衫
tào tóu shān jumper

4

汗衫　　　裤子　　　T恤　　　短袜

hàn shān vest　　　*kù zi* trousers　　　*tee shoo* t-shirt　　　*duǎn wà* socks

5

早餐 *zǎo cān* Breakfast

面包
miàn bāo bread

牛奶
niú nǎi milk

鸡蛋
jī dàn eggs

6

苹果　　　　　橙子　　　　　香蕉

píng guǒ　apple　　*chéng zi*　orange　　*xiāng jiāo*　banana

厨房 *chú fáng* The kitchen

桌子
zhuō zi table

椅子
yǐ zi chair

盘子
pán zi plate

刀子　　餐叉　　勺子　　杯子

dāo zi　knife　　*cān chā*　fork　　*sháo zi*　spoon　　*bēi zi*　cup

玩具　*wán jù*　Toys

马
mǎ　horse

羊
yáng　sheep

母牛
mǔ niú　cow

10

母鸡　　猪　　火车　　积木

mǔ jī hen　　*zhū* pig　　*huǒ chē* train　　*jī mù* blocks

拜访 *bài fǎng* On a visit

奶奶
nǎi nai Granny

爷爷
yé ye Grandpa

拖鞋
tuō xié slippers

12

外套
wài tào coat

连衣裙
lián yī qún dress

帽子
mào zi hat

公园　*gōng yuán*　The park

树
shù　tree

花
huā　flower

秋千
qiū qiān　swings

球
qiú　ball

14

滑梯
huá tī slide

靴子
xuē zi boots

鸟
niǎo bird

船
chuán boat

街道　　*jiē dào*　　The street

汽车
qì chē　car

自行车
zì xíng chē　bicycle

飞机
fēi jī　plane

卡车

kǎ chē truck

公共汽车

gōng gòng qì chē bus

房子

fáng zi house

聚会　*jù huì*　The party

气球

qì qiú　balloon

蛋糕

dàn gāo　cake

时钟

shí zhōng　clock

冰淇淋　　　　鱼　　　　饼干　　　　糖果

bīng qí lín　ice cream　　*yú*　fish　　*bǐng gān*　biscuits　　*táng guǒ*　sweets

19

游泳池 *yóu yǒng chí* The swimming pool

手臂
shǒu bì arm

手
shǒu hand

腿
tuǐ leg

脚　　脚趾　　头　　屁股

jiǎo　feet　　*jiǎo zhǐ*　toes　　*tóu*　head　　*pì gu*　bottom

21

更衣室　　*gēng yī shì*　　The changing room

嘴

zuǐ　mouth

眼睛

yǎn jing　eyes

耳朵

ěr duo　ears

鼻子
bí zi nose

头发
tóu fa hair

梳子
shū zi comb

刷子
shuā zi brush

23

商店　*shāng diàn*　The shop

红色　*hóng sè*　red

蓝色　*lán sè*　blue

绿色　*lǜ sè*　green

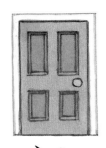   

门
mén door

书
shū book

洋娃娃
yáng wá wa doll

泰迪熊
tài dí xióng teddy

Match the words to the pictures

书
shū

靴子
xuē zi

火车
huǒ chē

洋娃娃
yáng wá wa

汗衫
hàn shān

鱼
yú

球
qiú

蛋糕
dàn gāo

母牛
mǔ niú

套头衫
tào tóu shān

时钟
shí zhōng

香蕉
xiāng jiāo

餐叉
cān chā

鸭子
yā zi

窗户
chuāng hu

猫
māo

狗
gǒu

牛奶
niú nǎi

短袜
duǎn wà

桌子
zhuō zi

苹果
píng guǒ

帽子
mào zi

灯
dēng

猪
zhū

冰淇淋
bīng qí lín

刀子
dāo zi

泰迪熊
tài dí xióng

汽车
qì chē

橙子
chéng zi

鸡蛋
jī dàn

31

数字 *shù zi* Numbers

1 一
yī one

2 二
èr two

3 三
sān three

4 四
sì four

5 五
wǔ five

1 一
yī
one

2 二
èr
two

3 三
sān
three

4 四
sì
four

5 五
wǔ
five

Reading *pinyin*

Almost all Chinese-English dictionaries, as well as this book, use the pronunciation system called *pinyin*. Read the *pinyin* words as if you were reading English, but:

h	has a harsher sound, like the Scottish *ch* in *loch*
q	sounds like the *ch* in *cheer*
x	sounds like the *s* in *see*
c	sounds like the *ts* in *cats*
z	sounds like the *ds* in *heads*

The next four are said with your tongue rolled back:

ch	sounds like the *ch* in *cheer*
sh	sounds like the *sh* in *shy*
zh	sounds like the *dge* in *fudge*
r	sounds like the *r* in *ring*

a	sounds like the *a* in *car*
an	sounds like the *an* in *can't*
e	sounds like the *e* in *the* or *mother*
en	sounds like the *en* in *shaken*
i	can sound like the *ee* in *seen*, or like the *i* in *shirt*, but
in	sounds like the *in* in *fin*
o	sounds like the *o* in *more*, and
ong	sounds like the *ung* in *sung*, but longer, more like *soong*
u	sounds like the *oo* in *too*
ü	for this sound, round your lips to say *oo*, then try saying *ee*

In Mandarin Chinese there are four tones, which means that the vowel sounds *a e i o u*, or groups of vowels, can be said in different ways:
1. The first tone is high and level.
    In *pinyin* it is written ˉ, as in *huā* (flower)
2. The second tone starts lower and then rises.
    It is written ´, as in *mén* (door)
3. The third tone starts in the middle, falls then rises.
    It is written ˇ, as in *wǔ* (five)
4. The fourth tone starts high and then falls.
    It is written ˋ, as in *shù* (tree)

Some vowel sounds, often in the second part of a word, are said without a particular tone and so are written without a tone mark. It is important to use the right tone because the same word can have very different meanings when said with different tones – for example, *mā* means "mother" but *mǎ* means "horse".

Word list

This list shows all the words in this book in the alphabetical order of the English words. Next are the Chinese words written in Chinese characters, then the *pinyin* guide to show you how to say them.

English	Chinese	Pinyin
apple	苹果	*píng guǒ*
arm	手臂	*shǒu bì*
baby	婴儿	*yīng ér*
ball	球	*qiú*
balloon	气球	*qì qiú*
banana	香蕉	*xiāng jiāo*
bath	浴缸	*yù gāng*
bathroom	浴室	*yù shì*
bed	床	*chuáng*
bedroom	卧室	*wò shì*
bicycle	自行车	*zì xíng chē*
bird	鸟	*niǎo*
biscuits	饼干	*bǐng gān*
black	黑色	*hēi sè*
blocks	积木	*jī mù*
blue	蓝色	*lán sè*
boat	船	*chuán*
book	书	*shū*
boots	靴子	*xuē zi*
bottom	屁股	*pì gu*
boy	男孩	*nán hái*
bread	面包	*miàn bāo*
breakfast	早餐	*zǎo cān*
brush	刷子	*shuā zi*
bus	公共汽车	*gōng gòng qì chē*
cake	蛋糕	*dàn gāo*
car	汽车	*qì chē*
cat	猫	*māo*
chair	椅子	*yǐ zi*

English	Chinese	Pinyin
changing room	更衣室	*gēng yī shì*
clock	时钟	*shí zhōng*
clothes	衣服	*yī fu*
coat	外套	*wài tào*
comb	梳子	*shū zi*
cow	母牛	*mǔ niú*
cup	杯子	*bēi zi*
Daddy	爸爸	*bà ba*
dog	狗	*gǒu*
doll	洋娃娃	*yáng wá wa*
door	门	*mén*
dress	连衣裙	*lián yī qún*
duck	鸭子	*yā zi*
ears	耳朵	*ěr duo*
egg / eggs	鸡蛋	*jī dàn*
eyes	眼睛	*yǎn jing*
feet	脚	*jiǎo*
fish	鱼	*yú*
five	五	*wǔ*
flower	花	*huā*
fork	餐叉	*cān chā*
four	四	*sì*
girl	女孩	*nǚ hái*
Grandpa	爷爷	*yé ye*
(father's father)	爷爷	*yé ye*
(mother's father)	外公	*wài gōng*
Granny	奶奶	*nǎi nai*
(father's mother)	奶奶	*nǎi nai*
(mother's mother)	外婆	*wài pó*
green	绿色	*lǜ sè*